Healthy Me

EAT RIGHT

Your Guide to Maintaining a Healthy Diet

by Allyson Valentine Schrier

Consultant:
Julie Negrin, M.S., C.N.
Culinary and Nutrition Educator
Author of *Easy Meals to Cook with Kids*
New York

CAPSTONE PRESS
a capstone imprint

Snap Books are published by Capstone Press,
151 Good Counsel Drive, P.O. Box 669, Mankato, Minnesota 56002.
www.capstonepub.com

Books published by Capstone Press are manufactured with paper
containing at least 10 percent post-consumer waste.

Library of Congress Cataloging-in-Publication Data
Schrier, Allyson Valentine.
  Eat right : your guide to maintaining a healthy diet / by Allyson Valentine Schrier.
    p. cm. — (Snap books. Healthy me)
  Summary: "An introduction to healthy eating habits, including the food pyramid, basic nutrition, and tips on making
healthy choices"—Provided by publisher.
  ISBN 978-1-4296-6544-5 (library binding)
  ISBN 978-1-4296-7291-7 (paperback)
  1. Nutrition—Juvenile literature. 2. Food—Juvenile literature. I. Title. II. Series.

RA784.S387 2012
613.2—dc22   2011002477

Editor: Mari Bolte
Designer: Juliette Peters
Media Researcher: Svetlana Zhurkin
Production Specialist: Laura Manthe

Photo Credits:
Capstone Studio: Karon Dubke, 5, 6, 7, 8, 12, 13, 15, 16, 17, 18, 19, 20, 21, 23, 24, 25, 26, 27, 28, 29 (bottom);
Dreamstime: Eugene Feygin, 22; iStockphoto: Barbara Reddoch, 29 (top); Shutterstock: Anna Subbotina, cover (bottom
left), ifong, 10, Laurent Renault, 14, Loskutnikov, cover (top left), Monkey Business Images, 9, Phil Date, cover (front),
Serghei Starus, cover (right)

Essential content terms are **bold** and are defined at the bottom of the page where they first appear.

Printed in the United States of America in North Mankato, Minnesota.
032011   006110CGF11

Table of Contents

Chapter 1
Small Changes, Big Differences 4

Chapter 2
Picture a Perfect Diet 8

Chapter 3
How Much Is Enough? 18

Chapter 4
What's in a Label? 22

Chapter 5
Is It Time to Eat Yet? 26

Glossary 30
Read More 31
Internet Sites 31
Index 32

Small Changes, Big Differences

Start the Day Off Right

What a morning! You snoozed through the alarm. Your hair has taken on a life of its own, and your shoes are playing hide-and-seek. You zoom to the kitchen for a quick bowl of cereal. But the bus is just around the corner. There's no time!

If you could change one thing, you'd have the mornings start later in the day. Then you could sit down to eat. Now it's too late for breakfast. You grab your backpack and leave the house hungry.

By mid-morning you're fading. Why are you so tired? You're sure your classmates can hear your stomach rumbling. Could one little thing like skipping breakfast make that big of a difference?

Healthy Tip

Here are some on-the-run choices that can start your day off with a full tank of healthy fuel:

- hard-boiled egg
- toast with peanut butter
- fruit and a handful of nuts
- yogurt

The bell finally rings for lunch. You race to the cafeteria. You've almost finished your pizza and chocolate milk when you overhear a couple of girls at the next table.

"Why do you drink skim milk?" one of them asks. "We always get 2-percent at our house."

"It's got all the same vitamins and stuff as 2-percent," says the other. "But it has fewer **calories**."

You know a bit about calories. You know that if you take in more calories than you burn off, you gain weight. Those girls seem pretty healthy. Would you feel healthier if you switched to skim?

calorie: a measurement of the amount of energy that food gives you

5

Breaded Chicken
Calories = 530
Total Grams of Fat = 20

Grilled Chicken
Calories = 420
Total Grams of Fat = 10

That night your family goes out to eat. You're about to order your favorite crispy chicken sandwich when you spot a nutrition chart on the wall. Whoa! You can't believe how many calories are in the sandwich.

"Make my sandwich grilled," you say. "And a salad instead of fries." When your food comes, you decide to make the switch to grilled chicken permanent.

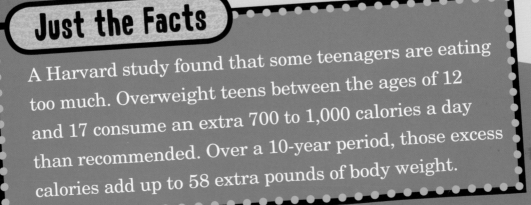

Just the Facts

A Harvard study found that some teenagers are eating too much. Overweight teens between the ages of 12 and 17 consume an extra 700 to 1,000 calories a day than recommended. Over a 10-year period, those excess calories add up to 58 extra pounds of body weight.

Before you go to bed, you pour yourself a glass of milk. "Can you get skim next time you're at the store?" you ask your mom. "I'd like to try to be a little healthier."

You feel good about the choices you made today. You can't change the sunrise, but you can change what you put into your body. Whether it's missing breakfast or choosing to go low-cal, little changes can make a big difference in how you feel.

Chapter 2

Picture a Perfect Diet

Fueling Your Body

Like cars, your body needs fuel. A car with low-quality gasoline won't run as well. It's the same with your body. Knowing how to tell good fuel from bad can help you choose the best way to rev up your engine.

A healthier diet doesn't mean giving up everything you love. Making one better choice each day is the way to grow a healthier you. Instead of skipping breakfast, eat something quick and easy. Say no to sugary drinks. If you still want a soft drink, make it a small instead of a large. And if potato chips are your weakness, choose baked instead of fried.

Healthy Tip

Eating food made from scratch is a great way to start your healthy lifestyle. Prepackaged foods such as popcorn or soup are full of salt, sugar, and additives. When you make it yourself, you know exactly what's in it!

There are five food groups—grains, vegetables, fruits, dairy, and proteins, such as meat and beans. Each group is important. A healthy diet draws from each group, every day. Your body needs the **nutrients** each group provides.

However, many people do not get enough of the right foods. The average person gets less than 60 percent of the recommended amount of vegetables. Most people also don't get enough fruit, whole grains, and dairy products.

nutrient: a substance needed by a living thing to stay healthy

The 2010 USDA dietary guidelines recommend a number of changes in the average Americans' diet. Here are a few steps for making the right choices at breakfast, lunch, and dinner:

- focus on a more plant-based and **fiber**-filled diet. Add more vegetables, fruits, nuts, seeds, and whole grains to your diet.
- choose low-fat or fat-free dairy products.
- eat meat in moderation and add more seafood to your diet. Stick to eggs, lean meats, and poultry.
- eat fewer foods made with solid fats, lots of sodium, added sugar, or refined grains.

fiber: a part of food that passes through the body but is not digested

Get Your Grains

You eat grains, such as rice, oats, wheat, and corn, every day. They can be eaten whole or be ground into flour. You see them in foods such as tortillas, noodles, and breakfast cereals. Breaded foods, such as chicken nuggets, fish sticks, and corn dogs, are coated in flour. Some surprising foods also contain wheat, including soy sauce or ketchup.

Whole wheat bread is made with whole grains. That means the entire wheat berry was used to make flour. Whole grain bread is high in fiber, vitamins, and minerals. High-fiber foods help prevent **diabetes** and heart disease too.

Make sure the bread you eat is actually whole grain. If the label says "100 percent whole wheat" then you've made a good choice. Labels claiming "100 percent wheat" don't guarantee that your bread is whole grain.

White bread is made with refined grains. The refining process gives the food a finer texture and extends the food's shelf life. But refining also removes many important nutrients such as fiber and iron.

Try to choose grains that look whole and natural, such as rice, flax, wheat berries, and oats. Avoid grain-based foods that have been refined and ground down. Make sure at least half of what you eat is made from whole grains.

diabetes: a disease in which there is too much sugar in the blood

Greens are Good!

It's a fact—people who eat lots of veggies are healthier than people who don't. That's because vegetables are full of fiber, vitamins, and minerals. Any vegetable falls into this category. And they all have great benefits. Want skin so healthy it glows? Veggies high in vitamin A will give you that shine. Spinach, collards, and carrots are high in vitamin A. This vitamin is also great for your eyesight, bones, teeth, and lungs.

Got a scrape or cut? Red and green peppers, orange squash, broccoli, and cauliflower are packed with vitamin C. This important vitamin boosts your **immune system** and helps your body heal.

immune system: the part of the body that protects against germs and diseases

Most Americans do not get enough vitamins or minerals. This fact is partly due to not eating enough fruit and vegetables. But much of the soil we use to grow food is losing nutrients too. This means fruit and vegetables contain fewer vitamins and minerals than in the past.

Juicy Fruits

Craving a sweet treat? Head to the fruit basket instead of the cookie jar. Crisp apples, juicy plums, and plump grapes have natural sugars. The body digests these natural sugars much easier than refined sugars. Fruit also has lots of fiber and water, which help you feel fuller for longer time periods. Like veggies, fruit is rich in vitamins. Oranges, mangoes, and strawberries are swimming in vitamin C. Watermelon, cantaloupe, and grapefruit are full of vitamin A.

Eat a rainbow every day for the richest mix of vitamins. Don't be afraid to try new kinds of fruit and veggies.

Healthy Yellow Oils

To keep your body running smoothly include some healthy oil in your diet. Healthy oils are found in plant foods, like nuts and seeds. Fats that are liquid at room temperature, such as sunflower, sesame, or olive oil, are good fats.

Steer clear of fats that are solid at room temperature. These saturated fats are found in meats, dairy products like cream or butter, and oil like coconut or palm.

One common solid fat to watch out for is trans fat. It is found in many snacks, fried foods, and baked goods. Look for the word "hydrogenated" on foods with trans fats. Hydrogenated fat is cheaper and has a longer shelf life than other fats.

Craving Calcium

Your body has 206 bones, and every one of them needs **calcium** to stay strong. Your bones store 99 percent of your body's overall calcium. If your body is low on calcium, it may "borrow" extra calcium from your bones. Too much borrowing and not enough replacing may lead to brittle bones later in life.

Milk is high in calcium, so make it a daily habit. Pour it on your breakfast cereal, grab a carton to sip with lunch, and drink it with dinner. Not a big milk drinker? Try other dairy products instead, such as yogurt or cheese.

Healthy Tip

Some people aren't able to digest lactose, the sugar found in milk and milk products. But being **lactose intolerant** doesn't mean you can't keep your body healthy. Tofu, almonds, and leafy greens, such as kale and Chinese cabbage, are also good sources of calcium.

calcium: a soft mineral needed for strong teeth and bones

lactose intolerant: the inability to digest lactose

Protein Is Everywhere

If you're craving meat, you're in luck. Meat is loaded with **protein**, which helps build strong muscles. But choose the leanest meats possible. Pork, chicken, and fish have less fat than beef. If you still want red meat, go for buffalo, venison, or lean cuts of beef such as top sirloin or eye of round. Many stores and farmer's markets now sell grass-fed beef, which is also a healthier choice.

Eggs are also another great source of protein. Don't forget to toss a few eggs into your diet. At breakfast, that extra punch of protein will help you stay energized until the lunch bell rings.

protein: a substance found in all plants and animals

It's also important to get a variety of proteins in your diet. Beans are excellent sources of protein and fiber. Give black, pinto, and even lima beans a chance! Grains such as quinoa, wild rice, or oats are good choices. So are nuts and seeds.

Just the Facts

The recommended portion size for meat is 5 ounces (142 grams). But be careful! The average fast-food burger is nearly that size—and that's just the most basic burger. Upgrading beyond that can easily double or triple the amount of beef.

Chapter 3

How Much Is Enough?

Now you know that you're supposed to choose food from each food group. But how many servings are enough, and what does a serving look like?

Grains: 6 servings

Great at meal or snack time! A serving could be:

- a slice of 100-percent whole-grain bread
- 1 cup (240 mL) of 100-percent whole-grain cereal
- 1/2 cup (120 mL) of 100-percent whole-grain oatmeal, pasta, or rice
- 3 cups (720 mL) of plain popped popcorn

Tip: 8 ounces (227 gm) is the same as 1 cup.

Veggies: 5 half-cup servings

Getting five servings of veggies is easier than you think. Sneak them into foods you love. Chop them up and add them to salads, soups, and scrambled eggs. Dive into a spinach salad or sautéed greens. Try veggie pizza instead of pepperoni or sausage. Here are a few ways to fit in a half-cup serving:

- one full-sized carrot
- one stalk of celery
- one small ear of corn
- half of a small potato

Fruits: 3 half-cup servings

Fresh is best, but frozen, dried, or juiced counts too. One half-cup of fruit could come from:

- four large strawberries
- half a grapefruit
- 16 grapes
- one 4-oz. (113-gm) container of applesauce

Milk: 3 cups

Drink a carton of milk with lunch and you're one-third of the way there! Other one-cup choices:

- one 8-oz. (227-gm) container of yogurt
- three domino-sized pieces, or 1.5 oz. (43 gm) of cheese
- a cup of frozen yogurt

What You're Eating vs. What You Should Be Eating

Calories from solid fats and added sugars

35%

65%

Calories from nutrient-dense foods

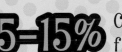 **5–15%** Calories from solid fats and added sugars

85–95%

Calories from nutrient-dense foods

Nutrient-dense foods are those prepared without adding solid fats or sugars.

Oils: 5 teaspoons

Most Americans get their daily allowance of oils from the foods they eat. Here are a few common sources of oils:

- a sandwich with 4 tablespoons (60 mL) of peanut butter has 4 teaspoons (20 mL) of oil
- 2 tablespoons (30 mL) of salad dressing has 2 teaspoons (10 mL) of oil
- a tuna sandwich made with 2 tablespoons (30 mL) of mayonnaise has 2½ teaspoons (12.5 mL) of oil
- 1 oz. of almonds (20-25 nuts) has 3 teaspoons (15 mL) of oil

Protein: 5 ounces

Picture a burger patty or piece of chicken as big as a deck of cards. That's about 3 ounces (85 grams). You're more than halfway there! Here are a few sources of protein to help you get to the 5-ounce mark:

- 1 large egg is 1 oz. (30 grams)
- a walnut-sized lump of peanut butter is 1 oz. (30 grams)
- a small can of tuna is 3 oz. (85 grams)
- a cup of pea or bean soup is 2 oz. (57 grams)
- 3 oz. (85 grams) of fresh fish, such as salmon, cod, or halibut

Exercise: 60 minutes a day

It's not just about what we eat. It's also about what we do when we're not eating. Exercise is a huge part of being healthy. It builds muscles and burns calories. How do you burn off that 155-calorie can of soda you couldn't say no to? Start with a half-hour of exercise. The amount you weigh will play a part in how many calories you burn during exercise.

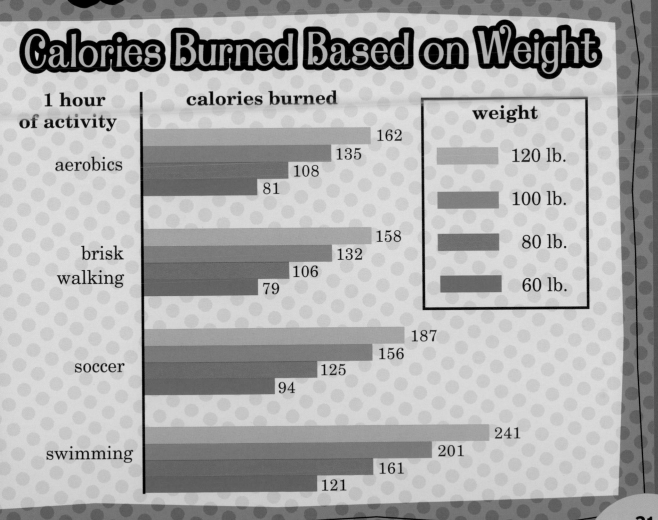

Calories Burned Based on Weight

1 hour of activity	calories burned				weight
aerobics	162	135	108	81	120 lb.
brisk walking	158	132	106	79	100 lb.
soccer	187	156	125	94	80 lb.
swimming	241	201	161	121	60 lb.

Chapter 4

What's in a Label?

Food packaging is full of labels. Zero Trans Fats! Sugar Free! Low-Fat! These words only tell part of the story. No fat? No sugar? People assume those labels make a food healthy. But a low-fat product may still have tons of sugar. One that claims to be sugar-free is likely sweetened with chemicals that are not the best for your body. The print on the front of the box can be confusing, misleading, or in some cases, false.

There's only one label that will tell you what's really in a product. Check out the black-and-white nutrition facts label found on the back or side of the product's box or bag.

Nutrition Facts

Serving Size 1 Bar (85g)
Servings Per Container 4

Amount Per Serving

Calories 170   Calories from Fat 50

	% Daily Value *
Total Fat 6g	**9%**
Saturated Fat 4g	**19%**
Trans Fat 0g	
Polyunsaturated Fat 0.5g	
Monounsaturated Fat 1g	
Cholesterol 13mg	**4%**
Sodium 83mg	**3%**
Total Carbohydrate 33g	**11%**
Dietary Fiber 4g	**16%**
Sugar 25g	
Protein 3g	

Vitamin A 110%	•	Vitamin C 2%
Calcium 10%	•	Iron 3%

*Percent Daily Values are based on a 2,000 calorie diet. Your daily values may be higher or lower depending on your calorie needs.

	Calories	2,000	2,500
Total Fat	Less than	65g	80g
Sat Fat	Less than	20g	25g
Cholesterol	Less than	300mg	300mg
		2,400mg	2,400mg
			375g
			30g

Healthy Tip

Avoid any food that has more than 400 calories per serving. A medium order of fries has 380 calories. Dunking your fries in ketchup can add another 15 calories per packet. A container of barbecue or honey mustard sauce adds about 50 or 60 calories.

The nutrition facts label shows the nutrients found in a single serving. A small bag of potato chips could contain two or more servings. A large bag could have as many as 12 servings. But a single serving might only be 12 chips, which makes overeating easy.

A good rule of thumb is to eat only one serving at a time. Find out exactly how much one serving is, and pour or scoop that much into a bowl. Eating out of the bowl will make it easier to stop once the single serving is gone.

When reading a nutrition facts label, there are things you should look for:

Look for:
- potassium
- fiber
- vitamins A and C
- iron
- calcium
- protein

Avoid:
- trans fat
- saturated fat
- cholesterol
- sodium
- sugars

The Ingredients List

You pick up a box of cereal and read the ingredients listed on the side of the box. The first ingredient listed is sugar. Ingredients are listed in order of weight, from most to least. This means that there is more sugar in this cereal than anything else.

When reading a product's ingredients list, here are a few tips to make smart choices:

• Choose foods where sugar is not one of the first ingredients.
• Look for foods where a whole grain is the first ingredient.

Ingredients to avoid:

• partially hydrogenated oil (trans fats)
• high fructose corn syrup
• foods you can't pronounce
• the word 'artificial'

Bring Home Healthier Choices

You can't drink skim milk if there's only whole milk in the fridge. Share what you know with the people who control what goes into the fridge.

• At the store, explain how to read labels.

• At the food shelf or food bank, take home whole grains, vegetables, and beans. These often go overlooked. They're easy to cook and super nutritious.

• At farmer's markets, you'll find food that is both fresh and local.

Just the Facts

Even if you don't see sugar on the ingredients list, there are other types of added sugars that can show up. Honey, syrups, and nectars are only a few names for sugar. Ingredients ending in -ose or including the word "malt" are usually also some form of sugar.

25

Chapter 5

Is It Time to Eat Yet?

Being your healthiest self isn't only about what you eat. It's about when you eat and why. Is it your stomach or your mood telling you to eat those cookies? Eating for the wrong reasons can lead to body issues like weight gain or **eating disorders**. Healthy eating habits include:

- eating only when you're hungry
- feeding your body, not your emotions
- avoiding eating while watching TV or when bored

eating disorder: a medical issue in which someone has a distorted view of his or her body and develops dangerous eating habits to lose weight

Just the Facts

It has been estimated that as many as 80 percent of all 13-year-olds have attempted to lose weight. Fifty percent of girls between the ages of 11 and 13 see themselves as overweight.

Ready, Set, Eat!

You're ready to start being the healthiest you've ever been—but wait a minute. How is anyone supposed to remember what you're supposed to eat and when? A cup of this, two slices of that, a handful of those. It's all so confusing! Relax. Don't let yourself get all tied up in the numbers. Here are the most important things to remember:

- Pick nutrient-dense foods. Choose snacks that pack the most fiber, vitamins, and other nutrients in a single serving.
- Avoid foods and drinks with no nutrition but lots of calories.
- Find your favorite whole-grain food.
- Choose low-fat meat and milk products.
- Fit veggies and fruits into every meal.
- Get moving! Try for at least 60 minutes of exercise every day.

Start small. Look for ways to make even one better choice each day. Remember, changing one small thing can make a big difference in how you feel.

Healthy Tip

If you find nutrition labels hard to follow, then try this on for size—just eat foods with no packaging at all! Fresh meat, fish, beans, vegetables, and fruit are the best things for our bodies. They don't need labels to tell us what they are.

Glossary

calcium (KAL-see-uhm)—a soft mineral needed for strong teeth and bones

calorie (KA-luh-ree)—a measurement of the amount of energy that food gives you

diabetes (dy-uh-BEE-teez)—a disease in which there is too much sugar in the blood

eating disorder (EE-ting dis-OR-duhr)—a medical issue in which someone has a distorted view of his or her body and develops dangerous eating habits to lose weight

fiber (FY-buhr)—a part of foods such as bread and fruit that passes through the body but is not digested; fiber helps food move through the intestines.

immune system (i-MYOON SISS-tuhm)—the part of the body that protects against germs and diseases

lactose intolerant (LAK-tohs in-TOL-er-uhnt)—the inability to digest lactose; lactose is the sugar found in milk and milk products

nutrient (NOO-tree-uhnt)—a substance needed by a living thing to stay healthy

protein (PROH-teen)—a substance found in all living plant and animal cells; foods such as meat, cheese, eggs, beans, and fish are sources of dietary protein

Read More

Hardyman, Robyn. *Eating Well.* Healthy and Happy. New York: PowerKids Press, 2012.

Schwartz, Heather E. *Make Good Choices: Your Guide to Making Healthy Decisions.* Healthy Me. Mankato, Minn.: Capstone Press, 2012.

Sohn, Emily. *Food and Nutrition: Eating to Win.* Iscience Readers. Chicago: Norwood House Press, 2011.

Internet Sites

FactHound offers a safe, fun way to find Internet sites related to this book. All of the sites on FactHound have been researched by our staff.

Here's all you do:

Visit *www.facthound.com*

Type in this code: 9781429665445

Super-cool stuff! Check out projects, games and lots more at **www.capstonekids.com**

Index

calcium, 15, 23
calories, 5, 6, 19, 21, 22, 28
choices, 4–7, 29

dairy products, 5, 7, 9, 10, 14, 15, 19, 25, 28
diabetes, 11

eating disorders, 26
exercise, 21, 28

fiber, 10, 11, 12, 13, 17, 23, 28
food groups, 9
fruit, 4, 9, 10, 12, 13, 19, 28, 29

grains. See whole grains

heart disease, 11
high fructose corn syrup. *See* sugars
hydrogenated fats. *See* oils

ingredients lists, 24, 25

lactose intolerance, 15

meat. *See* protein
milk. *See* dairy products
minerals, 11, 12

nutrient-dense foods, 19, 28
nutrients, 9, 11, 23, 28
nutrition labels, 6, 22, 23, 25, 29

oils, 14, 19, 20, 22, 23, 24

portions. *See* serving sizes
proteins, 9, 10, 14, 16–17, 20, 23, 25, 28, 29

saturated fats. See oils
seafood, 10, 16, 29
serving sizes, 8, 17, 18–20, 22, 23, 28
sodium, 8, 10, 23
sugars, 8, 10, 13, 19, 22, 23, 24, 25

trans fats. *See* oils

USDA dietary guidelines, 10

vegetables, 9, 10, 12, 13, 18, 25, 28, 29
vitamins, 5, 11, 12, 13, 23, 28

whole grains, 9, 10, 11, 17, 18, 24, 25, 28